# USING COMPUTER SCIENCE IN
# HIGH-TECH SECURITY
# »CAREERS«

CARLA MOONEY

Rosen
YA™

New York

Published in 2020 by The Rosen Publishing Group, Inc.
29 East 21st Street, New York, NY 10010

Copyright © 2020 by The Rosen Publishing Group, Inc.

First Edition

**Library of Congress Cataloging-in-Publication Data**

Names: Mooney, Carla, 1970– author. Title: Using computer science in high–tech security careers / Carla Mooney. Description: First edition. | New York : Rosen Publishing, 2020. | Includes bibliographical references and index. | Audience: Grades 7–12. Identifiers: LCCN 2018051776| ISBN 9781508187134 (library bound) | ISBN 9781508187127 (pbk.) Subjects: LCSH: Computer security—Vocational guidance—Juvenile literature. | Computer networks—Security measures—Vocational guidance—Juvenile literature. Classification: LCC QA76.9.A25 M678 2020 | DDC 005.8023—dc23
LC record available at https://lccn.loc.gov/2018051776

*Manufactured in China*

# CONTENTS

# INTRODUCTION

I n the 1990s, Jeff Williams became an application security engineer, taking this high-tech security position long before most people had heard of the career. "General Electric came to my company and said, 'We like your data centers, but we need every line of code reviewed for security before it goes on the internet,'" he said in an interview for CSO Online. "The sales team quickly said, 'Sure!' Everyone else took a quick step backwards and I got the job of figuring out how to deliver."

Application security is the practice of adding features or functions to software and web applications to reduce vulnerabilities and block threats. Threats include cyberattacks, network breaches, and data theft. To protect applications, application security engineers use firewalls, antivirus programs, encryption programs, and other features that prevent unauthorized access.

Application security is part of a company's overall high-tech security plan, which also includes system, network, and mobile security. The goal of the entire security plan, including application security, is to protect organizations and software users from hacking and other malicious intrusions. In his role as an application security engineer, Williams learned how to perform penetration testing and security code reviews, create application security architectures, complete threat modeling, and more.

An information technology engineer adjusts a wire connection in a company's server room. She is one of the professionals responsible for protecting the company's computer systems.

Today, Williams is the chief technology officer and cofounder at Contrast Security, a Palo Alto, California, application security vendor. He says that to be successful in this high-tech security career, people should have strong computer science skills and experience in multiple programming styles and languages. "But that's not enough," he said in an interview for CSO Online. "I look for people who work on open source projects, write their own tools, and code every day—those people that are excited and passionate about code. So, it's a lot more about real-world experience than book learning."

Technology is changing many aspects of daily life, from how people do business to how they communicate. Increasingly, organizations are relying on digital systems to generate, process, and store valuable information. The need to protect an organization's digital systems and data from unauthorized access and malicious hackers has given rise to new career fields in cybersecurity.

Cybersecurity is the protection of internet-connected systems, including hardware, software, and data, from breaches and cyberattacks. As companies are increasingly needing to protect their digital systems and assets, they require the skills of security professionals who combine technical skills with coding knowledge. Computer forensics, security engineering, security architecture, and cryptography are just a few examples of areas within cybersecurity that benefit from computer science and coding skills. The demand for information technology (IT) professionals with cybersecurity and technical skills is creating new opportunities for people with an interest in computer science and high-tech security. "Behind every new hack or data breach, there's a company scrambling to put out the fire. That's good news for job seekers with cyber security skills. Employers can't hire them fast enough," wrote journalist Jeff Kauflin in an article about high-tech security careers for *Forbes*.

In high-tech security, there are many different career specialties using computer science that students can pursue. Companies employ computer forensic specialists, security engineers, cryptographers, information security analysts, penetration testers, security architects, and more. With so many opportunities, careers that merge high-tech security and computer science can fit many backgrounds and interests.

# CHAPTER ONE

# PROTECTING DIGITAL ASSETS AND INFORMATION

Every day, organizations face threats to their information systems and data. Sophisticated attackers search for any weakness in an organization's systems and devise ways to exploit it. When they are successful, it can mean a simple interruption of services or a serious concern that sensitive data is being tampered with and sold. As more everyday objects are connected to the internet, from smart refrigerators to fitness trackers, the need for high-tech security to protect digital assets, systems, and information is greater than ever.

## WHAT IS CYBERSECURITY?

When people want to protect the valuables in their home, they install physical locks and security systems to prevent thieves from entering. Organizations that need to protect valuable digital systems and information turn to cybersecurity.

We are increasingly a highly connected society. Internet-enabled devices such as smartphones and fitness trackers are vulnerable to cybersecurity attacks.

Cybersecurity is the practice of making sure digital information, networks, and systems are safe from theft, manipulation, and other damage. Some damage can be accidental, such as when a hard drive fails or a natural disaster strikes. Increasingly, however, damage is caused by an intentional attack from a malicious entity. This includes individual hackers who are just trying to see if they can break into a system and organized criminal groups that steal data and information for financial gain.

Years ago, cybersecurity was mainly associated with government agencies and defense contractors. Today, all organizations need to address cybersecurity. Companies in industries such as health care, manufacturing, finance, retail, and more all employ cybersecurity professionals to protect valuable assets and information.

## TYPES OF CYBERSECURITY

Cybersecurity includes several types of high-tech security. Application security involves detecting vulnerabilities and developing tools and procedures to protect hackers from using weaknesses in an application to gain unauthorized access to company systems. Information security protects information and data from unauthorized access, breaches, manipulation, theft, and more. Network security involves monitoring an organization's internal networks to identify any weaknesses and prevent unauthorized access. Network security uses both hardware and software technologies, such as firewalls and antivirus and antispyware software, to keep internal networks secure and reliable.

Cybersecurity also involves planning for a disaster, whether natural or technical. This planning involves assessing and analyzing risks, prioritizing assets, and creating a disaster response plan. With a disaster plan in place, organizations can recover more quickly from a disaster and minimize any losses.

A website is another place where organizations can be vulnerable to attack. In recent years, there

Cybersecurity professionals work in a company server room and monitor a software program that detects any unauthorized access to the company's network.

has been a rise in the number of data breaches on websites. These breaches result in identity theft and financial losses for customers and companies. When a breach is made public, companies also suffer damage to their brand image and reputation. Website security focuses on protecting websites from online threats. It uses techniques and tools such as website scanning and malware removal, application security testing, website application firewalls, and more.

Mobile technology and the internet allow people to work from anywhere in the world. This flexibility also brings some risk since remote workstations and mobile devices are vulnerable to cyberattacks.

# COMMON CYBER THREATS

No organization—regardless of its size, industry, or location—is immune to cyberattacks. Understanding some of the most common threats can help cybersecurity professionals better design an organization's cyber defenses. Five of the most common threats faced by organizations include:

- **Socially engineered malware:** This type of attack tricks users into downloading harmful software onto a computer; the software can then spread to and disrupt a connected system or network.
- **Phishing attacks:** Password phishing attacks trick users into revealing their passwords and log-in information, which is then used to access an organization's network without permission.
- **Unpatched software:** Unpatched software contains vulnerabilities that allow hackers a point of access into an organization's network.
- **Social media threats:** Hackers can use social media accounts to gather information about a company and its employees, eventually piecing together enough information to successfully hack into the company's network.
- **Advanced persistent threats:** These frequently use phishing attacks or a Trojan attachment that delivers malware when opened to gain access to an organization's network and steal intellectual property.

When mobile devices connect to an organization's network and are interconnected, they create new entry points for hackers to gain access to a company's systems. Endpoint security protects and secures an organization's network by blocking attempts to access it from remote entry points.

## HIGH-TECH SECURITY AND COMPUTER SCIENCE

As more information and systems are connected online, there is a growing need for people who are interested in working in high-tech security and also have an interest in computer science and coding. According to ISACA, a nonprofit information security advocacy group, there is a global shortage of approximately two million cybersecurity professionals. In the United States, employers are struggling to fill cybersecurity jobs, with thousands remaining open because companies cannot find qualified professionals to fill them. There are needs for people to design and build security systems, try to break systems and identify weaknesses, monitor systems and detect intrusions, encrypt sensitive data, and more.

People interested in cybersecurity careers should have a strong background in computer science and understand how computers and software work. "Much of applied computer science is about solving problems with layers of abstraction, and security is often about finding the flawed assumptions in those abstractions

Knowing several programming languages and being able to code are useful skills for professionals who want to work in the cybersecurity field.

... and then figuring out how to best fix (or exploit) them," said cybersecurity expert Parisa Tabriz in a blog post for freeCodeCamp.

People working in cybersecurity can benefit from a knowledge of operating systems, networking, and computer architecture. Knowledge of security topics in networking, privacy enhancing technologies, and application security are also important to have. An understanding of some programming languages— such as Python, C, Java, JavaScript, PHP, HTML, and SQL—is valuable.

# PURSUING A CAREER IN HIGH-TECH SECURITY AND COMPUTER SCIENCE

There is no single path to a career in cybersecurity. Some people enter the field right out of college, while others gain experience working first in another IT position. No matter which path a person takes, all cybersecurity careers require a good foundation of general IT experience. People interested in this career field need to understand how technology works before they can learn how to protect it. Many choose to get a degree in computer science or information science from a four-year college, taking classes in operating systems, networks, programming languages, databases, and more. Classes in security topics are also beneficial. Some cybersecurity careers require advanced degrees, such as a master's degree or doctorate in IT with a focus on cybersecurity. For some positions, earning a certificate is a good way to show that a person has the technical skills needed for the career.

After earning a degree, cybersecurity professionals work in companies of all sizes, in almost every industry. Many work for consulting companies that perform services for a portfolio of clients. Others work in a company's internal IT department. Some cybersecurity professionals are self-employed, working on a freelance basis for clients.

In addition to taking classes, people interested in a high-tech security and computer science career can take other steps to learn more about the profession. Joining a cybersecurity professional organization can help a person learn more about the field and make contacts. Some companies offer internships to students. Internships give students the experience of working for a particular company or industry. Reading newspapers and other business and technology publications can help students keep up to date on the latest in cybersecurity.

For people who have an interest in security and computer science, a career in cybersecurity can be a challenging but rewarding choice. "It's not perfect. It will never be perfect. But I think the cutting edge of security is a lot better than it was 10 years ago, we can do some pretty impressive stuff with some level of reasonable assurance, and that's something that keeps me optimistic," said Tabriz in a blog post for freeCodeCamp.

# CHAPTER TWO

# DETECTIVES OF THE CYBER WORLD

A business owner learns that one of his employees is secretly planning to leave the company. He suspects that the employee is going behind his back and trying to take several of the company's clients with him to his new job. How can the owner find out if his suspicions are true? He turns to the detectives of the cyber world—computer forensic specialists. These cybersecurity professionals look through the employee's actions on company computers, systems, and online to see if they can find any incriminating evidence. If they do, the owner can use it to confront the employee.

## CYBER DETECTIVES ON THE CASE

Computer forensics is a branch of forensics, the use of scientific tests or techniques in the investigation of a crime. Computer forensic experts collect, analyze and present digital evidence in a crime investigation. They uncover information on computer systems, hard drives, CDs, and other storage devices. They comb through electronic documents and files such as emails and images. In many cases, digital evidence can be extremely difficult to find and gather because it is hidden or deleted. To find it, computer forensic experts use various software programs and other applications to uncover and extract latent or hidden data in a computer's systems. They work with many types of companies and organizations, including government agencies, accounting firms, law firms, banks, and software development companies. Any organization

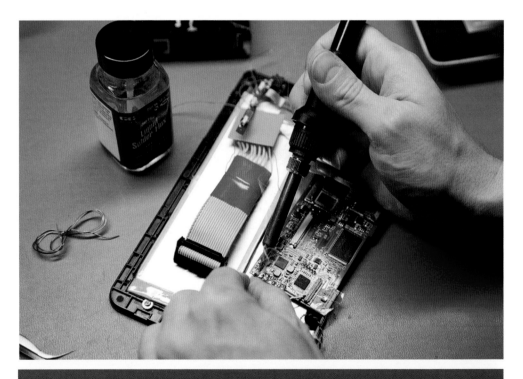

A computer forensics expert solders a piece of wire to a motherboard that will be attached to a computer to collect digital information for an investigation.

with a computer system may need the services of a computer forensic specialist.

Alfred Demirjian is the president and chief executive officer of computer forensics company TechFusion. Over his thirty years in computer forensics, he has been hired for many scenarios. In one case, he uncovered evidence of an employee sabotaging a former employer by hijacking an email account. In other cases, he has gathered evidence of employees misusing the internet while at work. Using forensic software, Demirjian can dig deep into an employee's social media postings and texts. He can sift through company emails during a specific date range to find evidence of an employee's interactions with clients and others. He can even track the employee by GPS if he or she has a company-owned smartphone. "Computer forensics will play a greater role in exposing the malicious acts of people. As it continues to advance, it will make it more difficult for people to hide their wrongful acts and easier to have them held responsible," Demirjian said in an article published in *CSO* magazine.

Every case that uses computer forensics is different. For example, a computer forensic specialist may be called in by law enforcement to help with the investigation of a person suspected of domestic terrorism. The specialist may be asked to identify and analyze all records of communication, internet activity, and data related to past or planned criminal activities. In another case, a computer forensic specialist may be called when an external hacker gains access to a corporate server that holds valuable information. The forensic specialist will determine how the hackers gained access to the server, if they accessed or stole data, and whether they introduced any malware or other hostile activity against the system.

## WORKING IN COMPUTER FORENSICS

People working in computer forensics combine a computer science background with forensic skills. They assist law enforcement and companies by collecting, analyzing, and presenting the digital data they uncover. The primary job of a computer forensic specialist is to find and collect the visible and hidden digital information on a computer system or other digital device. Sometimes, collection of data occurs on-site, at a suspect's home or office. More frequently, the devices to be examined are transported to a computer forensics lab for examination. Once the devices reach the lab, computer forensic specialists use a variety of technical tools to search for and collect data.

Computer forensic specialists analyze the data they collect. They explain what the data is, where it was recovered from, and what it might mean in a case to law enforcement and other investigators. Forensic specialists document each step they take during the recovery and analysis of digital data, so that the data can be used in court. Sometimes, the analysis of data can uncover new leads in a case and point the forensic specialist in a new direction.

Detective Shannon Geaney of the Los Angeles Police Department demonstrates computer forensics in a mobile lab, which is used to help the department investigate cyber crimes.

Once they have collected and analyzed data, computer forensic specialists typically prepare a written report of their findings. This report includes all discovered data that relates to the investigation. In some cases, computer forensic specialists may be called to share their report and findings in meetings or in court. "The best examination in the world is useless if you can't communicate clearly in a written report that can be easily understood by an agent, officer, lawyer, or jury," said John Irvine, a vice president at digital forensics and data recovery company CyTech, in an interview posted on the Balance Careers website.

According to Irvine, digital forensics is valuable because it provides information. He said in the interview posted on Balance Careers:

**Whether that information is evidence for a Federal**

## SUMMER CAMP WITH THE NATIONAL SECURITY AGENCY

While many teens are swimming, hiking, and toasting marshmallows, students at the National Security Agency (NSA)–sponsored summer camp at Marymount University learn how to crack encrypted passwords. At the computer, sixteen-year-old Ben Winiger typed a command into a software tool designed to help test and break passwords. "Now we're trying a brute-force attack," said Winiger in an article in the *New York Times*.

This GenCyber summer camp, and others like it around the country, teach middle school and high school students some of the skills they will need for future careers in cybersecurity. Each camp receives loose guidelines from the NSA and is free to decide which topics and exercises it will offer. According to the Marymount camp head Diane Murphy, an IT professor, her camp teaches students how to hack so that they can better defend against cyberattackers they might encounter in the future. NSA officials hope that camps like GenCyber for students will help build the next generation of computer forensics and cybersecurity professionals who will be needed to fill thousands of new cybersecurity jobs in the future.

criminal case or knowledge of an insider stealing corporate intellectual property for a competitor, digital forensics professionals provide data that the customers otherwise do not have available. In very simple terms, one could liken the job of a digital forensic examiner to that of a photo developer. For example, if I have an undeveloped roll of film in my hands, that's almost useless to me as any kind of evidence. However, if someone develops that film into pictures (or recovers data from a hard drive in our case), that content can provide everything the prosecutor, HR manager, or corporate security officer needs.

## HOW TO BECOME A COMPUTER FORENSIC SPECIALIST

For a career in computer forensics, most candidates earn a four-year degree from a college or university in IT, computer science, or a related field. In these programs, students learn about computer operating systems, networks, hardware, and software applications. Students can also take courses in accounting and criminal justice to learn skills they will need in a computer forensics career. High school students interested in computer forensics can take classes in computer science, programming, and accounting to prepare for this career.

While a few schools offer computer forensics programs, many forensics professionals learn advanced investigative techniques and skills on the job. "Computer Forensics is an apprenticeship

College students majoring in computer science listen and take notes during a lecture where they learn about different computer operating systems.

discipline," said Irvine in an interview posted on Balance Careers. "You really learn the trade once you're in a seat working on real cases alongside a senior examiner." In entry-level positions, computer forensic professionals can gain hands-on experience with hacking and intrusion techniques, security testing, and computer system diagnostic testing. In addition to strong technical skills, computer forensic professionals should have strong analytical skills, be detail oriented, and be able to juggle multiple projects and tasks at the same time.

Some employers require computer forensic professionals to be certified. Earning a certification demonstrates that the professional has mastered specific skills needed for the job. For computer forensic professionals, professional organizations such as the International Society of Forensic Computer Examiners and the International Association of Computer Investigative Specialists offer a Certified Forensic Computer Examiner certification. The certification must be renewed every three years.

## THE JOB OUTLOOK IN COMPUTER FORENSICS

The job outlook for computer forensics careers is expected to be very good. According to the Bureau of Labor Statistics (BLS), employment of information security analysts, which includes computer forensic professionals, is projected to grow 28 percent from 2016 to 2026. This rate of growth is much faster than the average growth rate of all occupations (7 percent). As more crime occurs online and cyberattacks increase in frequency, computer forensic professionals will be needed to uncover, analyze, and present this digital data for investigators and courts. In addition, computer forensic professionals will be needed to help organizations in many industries protect their computer systems from hackers.

Computer forensic professionals with related experience, a computer science degree, and a forensics certification will likely have the best chance at landing a good job in computer forensics.

# CHAPTER THREE

# PROTECTING COMPUTER NETWORKS

Every day, more information moves online, including financial records and Social Security numbers. As a result, organizations are becoming more vulnerable to data breaches, which occur when hackers attempt to break into an organization's databases and systems to steal information. Such break-ins are a growing problem and cost companies millions of dollars. According to the Ponemon Institute's *2017 Cost of Cyber Crime* report, security breaches are increasing. These breaches are costing organizations an average of $11.7 million per year. One of the most successful breaches in recent years occurred in 2017 when 147 million customer records were stolen from Equifax, a consumer credit reporting agency. The stolen records included customer names, birth dates, Social Security numbers, addresses, and more personal information.

Hackers do several things with the information they steal. They might sell it on the black market, use it to

A customer inserts a credit card into a payment machine. Information security analysts design solutions to keep customer personal information safe.

commit identity theft, or use it to directly steal from or otherwise take advantage of their victims. As a result, protecting the information generated by businesses, clients, and consumers has become an enormous task for companies across all industries.

## WORKING AS AN INFORMATION SECURITY ANALYST

Organizations hire information security analysts to guard and protect their information systems. These analysts plan security procedures and put security systems into effect. Their goal is to protect an organization's computer systems, networks, and data from cyberattacks, data breaches, and other unauthorized access or usage.

In a typical day, information security analysts will monitor an organization's networks, looking for signs of a breach. Signs include unusual data traffic patterns entering or leaving a company's network or changes in a privileged user's account activity. If analysts suspect a breach has occurred, they will investigate, resolve, document, and report the incident. These analysts also install firewalls and use data encryption programs to protect a company's data. They simulate attacks on the organization's networks to identify vulnerabilities that need to be fixed. They research the most up-to-date security procedures and products, develop an organization's long-term information security plan, and make recommendations about security to senior management. They also help the company's employees learn to use security products and procedures so they can avoid getting fooled by the many scams that hackers think up to gain access to confidential information.

Although all computer science professionals need to stay up-to-date on the latest industry trends, doing so is particularly critical for information security analysts. As soon as security analysts prevent one type of cyberattack, would-be hackers come up with schemes and tricks to launch another one. As a result, information security analysts need to know the latest types of attacks cybercriminals are launching and what technologies and techniques are being developed to

At a cybersecurity conference, hackers participate in a test to identify security weaknesses. This test will help information security professionals develop better cyber defenses.

combat them. To do this, they may attend conferences, where they meet with other professionals to discuss new attacks and protection strategies.

Part of this job involves creating a disaster recovery plan for an organization's data and computer systems. If a natural disaster strikes, the organization must be able to recover and restore operations as quickly as possible. This usually involves making regular copies of valuable data and transferring it to a secure, off-site location. Analysts also develop plans to restore computers and networks after a disaster.

According to information security professional Andrea Hoy, a typical day for her can involve many things. She initiates responses to potential threats, analyzes captured digital data for an investigation, and tests new code to ensure that it is secure. She also creates reports on her department's activities, such as the number of blocked phishing attacks for the month. Hoy also reviews the company's cybersecurity policies and procedures, evaluates new and existing cybersecurity tools, and answers questions about the implementation of new technologies. Her job keeps her busy and fulfilled. Hoy said in an article posted on the *U.S. News & World Report* website that "it provides great challenges on a daily basis."

## STEPS TO BECOME AN INFORMATION SECURITY ANALYST

Most information security analysts have at least a bachelor's degree from a four-year college or university in computer science, computer programming, or a related field. Some schools have specific programs for information security professionals. Some employers require candidates to have a master's in business administration in information systems.

Many employers prefer candidates who have related work experience, such as working as a network or systems administrator in an IT department. Organizations looking to hire a database security analyst may prefer a candidate

Information security analysts collaborate in a control center and listen to a supervisor give an update on the latest attempts to breach company networks.

who previously worked as a database administrator, while those looking to hire a systems security analyst may prefer a candidate who worked as a computer systems analyst.

Although there are no required certifications or licenses for information security analysts, some voluntary training and certifications can improve a person's chances of landing a job or getting promoted. Some certifications are general, while others specify areas such as penetration testing or systems auditing.

"While I don't feel you should spend all your time accumulating more letters behind your name, having a bachelor's degree and an entry-level certification can really separate you when looking for that first job," said Hoy in an article posted on the *U.S. News & World Report* website.

In addition to technical skills, successful information security analysts should have strong analytical, critical-thinking, and problem-solving skills.

## GETTING EXPERIENCE: A CYBERSECURITY INTERNSHIP

Working in an internship can help students gain valuable hands-on experience and build essential skills for information security careers. As an intern, Tiffany Smith worked for Foreground Security, a cybersecurity firm. Each intern was given an assignment: Smith's project was installing a monitoring tool called Opsview onto a Red Hat server. Smith spent long hours figuring out how to install the monitoring tool. "This was extremely challenging to me, but I figured it out by keeping track of the steps I took in every phase of installation," said Smith in a blog post on KeirstenBrager.tech. "This experience prepared me for the challenges I had waiting for me in my first full time cyber security role. My project was selected and placed into production of the company at the end of my internship and I was extremely ecstatic!"

the weaknesses and strengthen digital security before an outside hacker has the opportunity to breach the system, cause damage, and steal information. To do this, they may rewrite program code or add additional security technologies or procedures. When they perform testing, they document the results and findings in reports for company management.

## WORKING IN PENETRATION TESTING

Aleksander Gorkowienko and Steven van der Baan are penetration consultants at 7Safe, a cybersecurity consulting company. They spend most of their time attempting to break into companies' computer systems. Each client uses different technologies and presents a unique challenge. Sometimes Gorkowienko and van der Baan perform an SQL (Structured Query Language) injection, which places a query into a database that allows the hacker to manipulate it without authorization. Other times, they perform phishing attacks, which is when a hacker impersonates someone over the phone or via email and tries to get an employee to reveal information like security keys or passwords. Regardless of the method, the penetration testers try to find any weaknesses in their clients' systems to prevent a breach before it happens. "If there's a hole it will be found sooner or later—these days, sooner," said Gorkowienko in an article for *Computerworld UK*.

# CRACKING PASSWORDS AS AN INTERN

Students interested in penetration testing careers can gain valuable hands-on experience working in a security internship. In 2017, Tim Welles worked as a summer intern for Sword & Shield Enterprise Security, an information security consulting company. Welles, a student at the University of Tennessee majoring in computer science with a focus in cybersecurity, worked on a project to set up a programming function called a wrapper for a hashcat installation, a password cracking tool, in the company office. Welles said in an article on the Sword & Shield website:

> The hashcat wrapper for distributed hashcracking project was a perfect pick for an intern such as myself. It gave me something to do that I feel will add value back to this company well beyond my time there, and accomplish work they needed to be done. At the same time, it taught me a lot about password cracking and Linux in general, as well as some general networking skills. The best part of the project was when I finished and the team actually started using it in their penetration testing services. This made me feel like I was making an impact on the company vs. working on a side project that would not be utilized very much.

Welles plans to pursue a career in cybersecurity after he graduates.

For one client, van der Baan found a system where he could manipulate the database and read files from the underlying operating system. Another error he discovered gave him the system's code. When he downloaded it, he found a vulnerability that allowed him to execute whatever code he wanted—a weakness that could be very dangerous if found by a malicious hacker. "What we find and where we find it, what our end results are, completely depends on the system," he said in an April 2016 article for *Computerworld UK*. By showing the client these vulnerabilities, van der Baan was able to help the client understand where it needed to strengthen its cyber defenses.

Malicious hackers sometimes impersonate others over the phone to gain access to sensitive personal information, such as usernames and passwords.

# HOW TO BECOME A PENETRATION TESTER

For someone who is curious and has a talent for coming up with unique and sophisticated fixes for cybersecurity, a career in penetration testing may be a great fit. Most penetration testers have several years of relevant experience and at least a bachelor's degree in computer science, information security, or a related field. These programs prepare students with skills in programming, networking, and cybersecurity. Students will take courses in areas such as computer forensics, disaster recovery, penetration testing, and more. High school students can prepare for a career in penetration testing by taking computer science and programming courses.

Most careers in cybersecurity, including penetration testing, require strong technical and computer skills so that these professionals can hack into computer systems. Some employers require candidates to know specific programming languages, such as C, C++, Java, PHP, and Python. Because clients run different operating systems, penetration testers should know Windows, UNIX, and Linux operating systems. They should also have experience with web-based applications, network servers and networking tools, security tools, and security frameworks. Jeff Williams, chief technology officer and cofounder of Contrast Security, said in an April 2018 article for *Forbes:*

> You'll definitely need a deep understanding of the technology you are testing. You don't have

Teens attend a computer workshop where they learn how to write code and practice programming skills, which will be useful for a career in penetration testing.

to become an expert coder, but you should know enough to build simple applications using the technologies you want to test and comprehend the code for more complex apps. I suggest specializing in technologies that are widely used to build applications that people actually care about like Java, .NET and the major application frameworks.

Candidates should also have a thorough understanding of security defenses and vulnerabilities. "Understanding security defenses like encryption, authentication, authorization, cross-site request forgery (CSRF) tokens, session IDs, HTTP headers, encoding/escaping and logging is critical," said Williams in the *Forbes* article. He also recommends that candidates get practical experience finding and exploiting system vulnerabilities. Some employers also require penetration testers to earn ethical hacking or other technology security certifications.

Penetration testers must be up-to-date on the latest methods and technologies hackers use, as well as the new security technologies. To do this, they can attend conferences where they meet with other professionals to discuss new attacks and security strategies.

## THE JOB OUTLOOK FOR PENETRATION TESTERS

The job outlook for penetration testers is very good. According to the BLS's *Occupational Outlook Handbook*, employment of information security analysts, which includes penetration testers, is projected to grow 28 percent from 2016 to 2026. This growth rate is much faster than the average rate for all occupations.

As the threats from cyberattacks become more frequent and sophisticated, organizations will need to make sure their cyber defenses are up to the task. "We need to stop dealing with cyber-attacks after the damage is done. We need to have foresight and prevent them from occurring in the first place," said

US representative C. A. Dutch Ruppersberger in a December 2014 article for *U.S. News &World Report*. As a result, the demand for penetration testers will grow as companies hire them to find and fix security weaknesses before a security breach occurs. Williams said in the article for *Forbes*:

> The demand for skilled penetration testers will continue to rise. If you're the kind of person who thrives on learning about all different kinds of systems and businesses and would be bored working on a single application for years, penetration testing might be for you.

# CHAPTER FIVE

# DEVELOPING THE SECURITY ARCHITECTURE

All organizations need to protect their technology and computer networks. To do so, they must create a comprehensive strategy that includes security systems, policies, and procedures that work together seamlessly across an organization's different users, systems, networks, and other technologies. The security architect takes on this challenge, designing, building, and maintaining high-tech computer systems security for an organization.

## BUILDING A SECURE CYBER SYSTEM

Security architects are responsible for the overall strategy for all cybersecurity operations within an organization. Looking at the big picture, they design an organization's security structures to block malware and attempts by hackers to gain access to

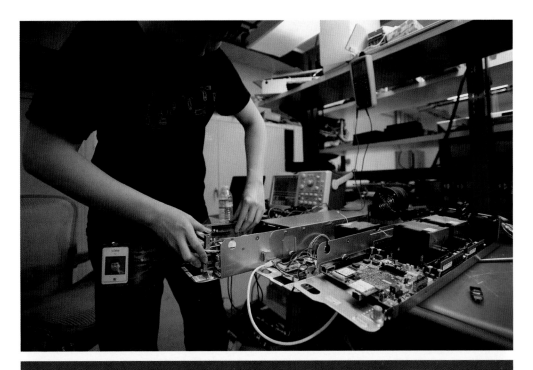

In order to design an organization's security system and overall security plan, security architects must understand all of the hardware and software used by the organization.

an organization's computer networks and systems. To do so, a security architect must have a thorough understanding of a company's technology and information systems. He or she should think like a hacker to understand and anticipate the tactics that hackers might use to gain access to computer systems. Knowing the systems and technologies used by the organization helps a security architect pinpoint who has access and where any security vulnerabilities may exist.

After making a comprehensive assessment of an organization's systems, the security architect plans, designs, and implements a security system using hardware and software. He or she researches security systems and protocols and develops requirements for networks, routers, firewalls, and other technologies. Often, the security architect delegates tasks to a team that will develop the code and other elements of the planned security system.

Once these systems and procedures are in place, architects test and audit the entire system for weaknesses. Sometimes, security architects work with penetration testers to run a complete test on a system's security to make sure its defenses will protect against outside attacks. If any issues are identified, security architects design and implement security fixes to resolve them. When a hacker tries to access the organization's systems, security architects set up countermeasures to protect the system and limit the hacker's ability to damage the system or steal valuable information.

In addition to designing and implementing security systems, security architects develop an organization's policies and procedures related to system security. They prepare training for employees to educate them about best practices to keep company systems safe.

Security architects must stay up to date on the latest technologies and security strategies so they can evaluate and improve an organization's security systems and keep it secure from threats. Because hackers are always coming up with new ways to infiltrate systems, security architects must also be aware of the latest hacking tactics so they can design solutions to block them.

A hacker sits in a dark room and uses the internet to break into a company's network and steal customer credit card information.

## WORKING AS A SECURITY ARCHITECT

As the security leader for a global organization, Michael Haag was responsible for cybersecurity strategy and architecture across many business units. As his company acquired new businesses, Haag and his colleagues worked to assess and design security programs and procedures for each. Haag said in an article posted on the Red Canary website:

**Our main goal here was understanding the risks we were accepting from the incoming organization.**

**We needed to understand how much exposure this organization had on the perimeter—open ports, vulnerable applications, Citrix gateways, and so on. It's important to identify these items as they are points of entry for threat actors ... Beyond this, we would also discuss patching strategies for operating systems and third-party software.**

According to Haag, no system is impenetrable. While security architects design systems and procedures to prevent hackers from gaining unauthorized access to an organization's networks and information, most organizations will experience a breach at some point. Security architects must be able to detect breaches and learn from them so they can be better prepared for the next hacker. "Prevention only goes so far," said Haag in the Red Canary article. "It can lead to a false sense of security ... something will be missed. I am a big believer in 'prevention is ideal; detection is a must.'"

## HOW TO BECOME A SECURITY ARCHITECT

Becoming a security architect involves a combination of education and experience. Most people pursuing a career as a security architect must have at least a bachelor's degree in computer science, IT, cybersecurity, or a related field from a four-year university or college. Many security architects also have a master's degree in cybersecurity or computer science with a security focus. High school students can prepare for a career in security architecture by taking computer science and programming courses.

Careers in security architecture require strong technical and computer skills. Security architects must be skilled in multiple operating systems—Windows, UNIX, and Linux. They are knowledgeable about network security and architecture, wired and wireless security, and enterprise and security architecture. They should also understand cryptography, distributed systems, and software design. They should be able to identify and model threats and risks to a system and be able to test for vulnerabilities.

Security architect Dawid Balut recommends that security architects learn to code. "Learn how software stacks work and get a handle on web programming languages like Java, PHP and their respective frameworks. To break something and improve its resiliency afterward, you should understand how it all works," he said in an article posted on the *Forbes* website.

A security architect is often a senior-level position in many companies. Therefore, most employers want to hire security architects who have three to ten years of relevant, on-the-job experience in IT and cybersecurity. Often, candidates work first in entry-level positions in network administration, security administration, and system administration to develop basic skills and knowledge. Then they progress to intermediate-level positions as security analysts, security engineers, or security consultants, in which they further develop computer security skills and gain hands-on experience they will need as a security architect. "I started my adventure in

Joe Steward, director of malware research at Dell SecureWorks, speaks with a security researcher in front of large monitors as they work to track internet hackers and criminals.

IT from the very bottom, working as a computer technician, network admin, web programmer, and system administrator," explained Balut in an article posted on the *Forbes* website. "My range of experience allows me to understand the problems many employees face, enabling me to make better decisions for the companies and teams I work with. I believe the security industry could benefit greatly from more diversity."

In addition, adding industry certifications to education and work experience can make a professional more appealing to employers. The

security hardware and software. They install and configure security software such as firewalls and data encryption programs. They install and process new security products such as software that notifies the team about unauthorized system intrusions. They develop automated code that tracks and reports on security incidents. When there is any change in an organization's hardware and software, security engineers are involved to ensure the changes do not expose the organization to new vulnerabilities.

Security engineers are also part of the security team that monitors networks and systems for breaches. They spend a lot of time looking for any system or network vulnerabilities and testing security solutions. To do this, they may conduct scans of networks or perform penetration testing. When a breach occurs, security engineers often lead the organization's response and investigate how the breach occurred. With this information, they install fixes to strengthen security.

Helen Oswell is a security engineer at 6point6, a technology consulting company. In her role, Oswell builds security systems and identifies ways to improve and eliminate vulnerabilities in a company's IT infrastructure. In an interview posted on the Learning People website, Oswell explained, "I work on tools and designs and work on structure papers during a normal day. My favorite part of the role is designing tools and implementing them—for example working on a vulnerability management tool in a cloud environment." She believes that it is more important than ever for companies to pay attention to their cyber defenses.

Security engineers work together to install updates to an organization's security firewall and data encryption programs.

While spending money on cybersecurity professionals can be costly, Oswell pointed out that "the real cost is when all your data gets hacked and your business can't function."

## HOW TO BECOME A SECURITY ENGINEER

Most security engineers have at least a bachelor's degree in computer or information science, computer programming, software engineering, or systems engineering. Students in these programs will typically

# THE PROPER CERTIFICATIONS

Earning a certification can show that a person has mastered important skills for security engineering. Some of the most popular certifications for security engineers include Certified Ethical Hacker, Cisco Certified Network Professional Security, and Certified Information Systems Security Professional. Students in these certification programs learn about hacker software, network security, computer forensics, cryptography, program testing, applied mathematics, and information system maintenance. Although many certifications are available, the process for obtaining each one is similar. Students must have a certain level of experience and pass an exam.

take courses in computer programming, networking, and systems design. Some companies prefer security engineers to have a master's degree, such as a master of science in information systems or a related field. Students in high school who want to become a security engineer can take classes in math, science, and computer science.

Security engineers must have strong technical and computer skills. They must know how to build security networks, including cloud systems. They should have experience using penetration and intrusion detection software, setting up firewalls, and configuring routers and software. While coding skills are not a requirement, they are helpful when engineers review code to search for security issues. Parisa Tabriz said in a blog post on freeCodeCamp:

> **The best security engineers I know are also actively writing code. This gives them firsthand experience with writing software, including unintentionally-yet-inevitably introducing security bugs. The latter forces a real empathy for all developers. After all, it's often harder to consistently write secure code than it is to point out insecure code.**

Security engineers should be familiar with operating systems such as Windows and Linux and database

A security engineer reviews code on a laptop and searches for any vulnerabilities or weaknesses in the code that will allow a hacker to breach an organization's software and systems.

security using MySQL, Oracle, and SQL Server. They should be able to use the latest encryption technology and networking security protocols such as TCP/IP and HTTPS. They should also keep up-to-date on the latest hacking techniques.

Those who work in this field need to keep up with the latest technologies and industry developments. To do so, they take continuing education courses throughout their careers and attend industry conferences.

# JOB OUTLOOK FOR SECURITY ENGINEERS

The job outlook for security engineers is very good. According to the BLS, employment of information security analysts, which includes security engineers, is projected to grow 28 percent from 2016 to 2026. While the demand for cybersecurity professionals, including security engineers, is soaring, the supply of qualified candidates is low. Research by the job site Indeed in 2017 found that although organizations have cybersecurity job postings, there are not enough candidates to fill them. Therefore, qualified candidates with related job experience will have their pick of jobs in security engineering.

# CHAPTER SEVEN

# ENCRYPTING DATA

I n 2013, computer software company Adobe announced that its computer systems had been hacked. Cyberattackers accessed millions of Adobe customer IDs, encrypted passwords, and encrypted credit or debit card numbers. The company later reported that hackers also stole the source code for Photoshop, its popular photo editing software. Thirty-eight million customers were affected by the breach.

While the breach and loss of data was very bad for Adobe, there was a tiny piece of good news. Some of the data stolen from the company was encrypted, including the customer passwords and debit and credit card numbers. Encrypting data is a method of concealing it with a code or cipher. That way, if unauthorized individuals access it, they cannot use or understand it. Because Adobe encrypted some of its data, only a portion of the stolen information had any value for the hackers. Encryption was one of the tools the company used to secure data stored in its systems. Rick Robinson, an industry expert in encryption and cryptography, said:

Data encryption software is one tool that can be used to protect an organization's data and prevent unauthorized users from accessing and reading it.

Today's enemies are data thieves working to steal your data for profit. If they cannot steal your data and profit from it, they will look elsewhere. Encrypted data represents an insurmountable challenge from which they cannot profit. Such use of encryption to protect your data and keep it from being used by perpetrators is a prime example of using cryptography for business.

# MAKING AND BREAKING CODES

When organizations need to encrypt and protect important data, they turn to cryptographers.

Cryptography is a method of protecting information and communications by using codes. Only those who are authorized to receive the information can read and process it. In today's digital world, cryptography typically scrambles ordinary text (also called plaintext) and turns it into ciphertext through the encryption process. Then cryptography turns ciphertext back into plaintext using a process called decryption. Businesses, military organizations, and government agencies use encryption and cryptography to protect data and networks from hackers and cyberterrorists. Professionals called cryptographers develop the algorithms, ciphers, and security systems used to encrypt valuable data. These algorithms are used to protect data, web browsing on the internet, and confidential communications such as email and credit card transactions.

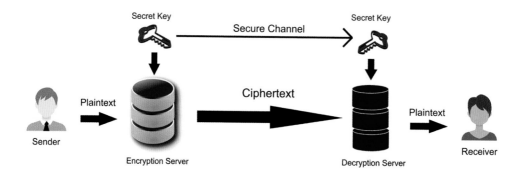

AES Algorithm Working

This illustration shows how a cryptographic algorithm can be used to encrypt and decipher data so that it can only be accessed by authorized users.

While every job in cryptography is different, cryptographers typically protect information from being intercepted, copied, modified, or deleted. They use mathematically based encryption methods. They write new algorithms to encrypt information like bank accounts and credit card information. Cryptographers analyze weaknesses in cryptographic security systems and algorithms and develop statistical and mathematical models to analyze data. Cryptographers also research and test new cryptography methods and applications. They search for vulnerabilities in an organization's communication systems—such as its wireless network, cell phones, and email—and ensure that communications are not illegally accessed or altered. In addition to encrypting sensitive data, cryptographers who work for military, government, and law enforcement agencies may also analyze and decode any hidden information in cryptic messages and coding systems.

Christof Paar has worked in applied cryptography since 1995 and is an affiliated professor at the University of Massachusetts–Amherst. According to Paar, cryptography is central to cybersecurity. "The cryptographic algorithm is the driving force, the heart, of almost every security solution," he said in an interview for IEEE Cyber Security. Paar has been working on applying cryptography to connected cars and vehicle-to-everything (V2X) communications, when a vehicle interacts with other vehicles (V2V) or with roadside infrastructure (V2I). V2V communication helps prevent collisions, while V2I communications can help reduce gridlock and pollution. Making sure these communications are secure and not altered in any way by hackers is essential. Paar said:

> Cryptography supports the authentication that allows these applications to trust one another, which obviously is key because they involve human lives in tons of metal moving at high speeds. Crypto algorithms are also a great way to encrypt V2X communications. An example is ensuring that a vehicle's real-time location information has not been manipulated. Without cryptography, it's possible

## TYPES OF CRYPTOGRAPHIC ALGORITHMS

There are three main categories of cryptographic algorithms:

- Secret key or symmetric encryption uses a single key for both encryption and decryption. It is primarily used to keep data private and confidential.
- Public key or asymmetric encryption uses one key for encryption and a different key for decryption. It is typically used for authentication.
- A hash function is an algorithm that can be run on data such as a file or password and produces a value called a checksum. The hash function can be used to verify the authenticity of a file or piece of data. If the checksums generated by two files are identical, one can assume the files are identical as well.

that a hacker could send fake message[s] that could cause, for instance, accidents by triggering automatic braking at high speeds.

# HOW TO BECOME A CRYPTOGRAPHER

For people who enjoy solving puzzles, advanced mathematics, and computer science, a career in cryptography may be appealing. Most cryptographer positions require candidates to have a bachelor's degree in mathematics, computer science, computer engineering, or a related field. Many also require a master's degree or doctorate in mathematics or computer science with a focus on cryptography. In addition, because they are working with highly sensitive data, some jobs require cryptographers to have high-level security clearances. High school students interested in cryptography can take classes in mathematics, statistics, computer science, and programming to prepare for this career.

Cryptographers need to have strong technical, mathematics, and computer skills. They should be familiar with computer architecture, data structures, and algorithms. They must understand linear/matrix algebra and discrete mathematics. Cryptography professionals should also be familiar with information theory, computer security, and engineering.

On the job, it is helpful to know several programming languages, such as C, C++, Python, and Java. Also essential are technical skills using the principles of symmetric and asymmetric cryptography, such as symmetric encryption, hash functions, key exchange, digital signatures, and more. "Today, cryptology professionals need to be gifted in both mathematical concepts and statistical analysis, coupled with a strong background in technology, to be able to make a career in this field," said computer security expert Gary C. Kessler in an article for the Bank Info Security website.

In addition to technical skills, cryptographers must be highly analytical and creative. To break complex codes, they must be able to think analytically and have a good understanding of mathematical theories so they can decipher coded information or create encryption systems that protect data. Even more importantly, cryptographers must have high ethical standards and good judgment because they are trusted with handling an organization's most sensitive data.

## THE JOB OUTLOOK FOR CRYPTOGRAPHERS

The job outlook for cryptography careers is expected to be very good. According to the BLS, employment of mathematicians and statisticians, which includes cryptography professionals, is projected to grow 33 percent from 2016 to 2026. The growth of e-commerce and the need for cryptographers to protect customer data online is one factor driving the demand for cryptographers.

As e-commerce continues to grow and more businesses move online, the demand for cryptography professionals will continue to be strong. "Data

Cryptography professionals use data encryption as one part of an overall cybersecurity plan to protect company and customer data from unauthorized access and use.

encryption and security is a huge and growing field today," said Rainer Steinwandt, associate director and coeditor of the *Journal of Mathematical Cryptology,* in an article for the Bank Info Security website. "New companies pop up daily that need to have data encrypted; they do that with software and 'keys' developed by cryptologists using mathematics." Cryptography professionals with related experience and a master's or doctoral degree in mathematics or computer science will likely have the best chance of landing a good job in the cryptography field.

**algorithm**  A process or set of rules to be followed in calculations, often by a computer.

**application**  A software program that runs on a computer.

**architecture**  A set of rules and methods that determines how a computer system functions and is organized.

**certification**  An official document that shows a level of achievement.

**cryptography**  The practice of solving or writing codes.

**cyberattack**  An attempt by hackers to damage a computer network or system.

**cybersecurity**  The process of protecting internet-connected computer systems, including hardware, software, and data.

**database**  A set of data held in a computer.

**data breach**  The intentional or unintentional release of private information to unauthorized users.

**e-commerce**  Commercial transactions that take place over the internet.

**encrypt**  To convert data into a code to prevent unauthorized access.

**firewall**  Part of a computer system or network that is designed to block unauthorized access.

**forensics**  Scientific tests and techniques used to investigate a crime.

**hacker**  A person who uses computers to gain unauthorized access to data or systems.

**identity theft**  The deliberate use of someone's identity, often for financial gain.

**internship**  A program in which a student or trainee works in an organization, sometimes without pay, in order to gain work experience.

**malicious**  Of or having an intent to do harm.

**malware**  Software that is meant to damage or disable a computer system or network.

**network**  A set of connected computers.

**source code**  Computer language designed to direct a software program.

**threat modeling**  The process identifying security risks by thinking like a hacker.

**vulnerability**  The ability to be attacked or harmed.

**Association of Information Technology Professionals (AITP)**

1120 Route 73, Suite 200

Mount Laurel, NJ 08054-5113

(800) 224-9371

Website: https://www.aitp.org

Twitter: @CompTIAAITP

The AITP works to advance the IT profession through professional development, education, and national policies. It features webinars, conferences, awards for professionals and students, a career center with a jobs board, and networking options that are of interest to computer science professionals.

**Association of Software Professionals (ASP)**

ASP Executive Director

PO Box 1522

Martinsville, IN 46151

(765) 349-4740

Website: http://asp-software.org

Facebook: @AssocSoftwareProfessionals

Twitter: @Applied_SW

The ASP is a professional trade association of software developers that provides a community for developers to share information about the industry.

**Canada's Association of Information Technology Professionals (CIPS)**

60 Bristol Road East

Unit 8, Suite #324

Mississauga, ON L4Z 3K8

Canada
(905) 602-1370
Website: http://www.cips.ca
Facebook: @CIPS.ca
Twitter: @cips
CIPS represents thousands of professionals in the
Canadian IT industry and provides networking
opportunities, certification of IT professionals,
accreditation of university and college programs,
and an IT job board. The organization also informs
the Canadian government about issues that affect
the IT industry and professionals in Canada.

## CompTIA
3500 Lacey Road, Suite 100
Downers Grove, IL 60515
(630) 678-8300
Website: https://www.comptia.org
Facebook and Twitter: @CompTIA
CompTIA provides many IT certifications and education
resources for professionals in IT. The organization
also advocates for the IT industry at the local,
state, and federal government levels.

## IEEE Computer Society
3 Park Avenue, 17th Floor
New York, NY 10016
Website: https://www.ieee.org
Facebook: @ieeecomputersociety
Twitte: @ComputerSociety
The IEEE Computer Society is the world's largest
professional organization for advancing technology

and engineering globally. It provides many publications, conferences, technology standards, and professional and educational activities that those interested in software development will find useful.

**Information Systems Security Association (ISSA)**
1964 Gallows Road, Suite 310
Vienna, VA 22182
Email: http://www.issai.org/en_us/site-issai
/other-information
Website: http://www.issai.org
Facebook: @ISSAIntl
Twitter: @ISSAINTL
The ISSA is a not-for-profit, international organization of information security professionals. It provides publications, educational forums, and networking opportunities for information security professionals.

**Information Technology Association of Canada**
5090 Explorer Drive, Suite 510
Mississauga, ON L4W 4T9
Canada
(905) 602-8345
Website: http://itac.ca
Twitter: @ITAC_Online
The Information Technology Association of Canada supports the development of a digital economy in Canada. It represents IT professionals in a wide variety of industries.

International Web Association (IWA)
556 S. Fair Oaks Avenue, #101-200
Pasadena, CA 91105
(626) 449-3709
Website: http://iwanet.org
The IWA is the industry's recognized leader in providing educational and certification standards for web professionals. The association supports more than 300,000 individual members in 106 countries.

**National Association of Programmers**
PO Box 529
Prairieville, LA 70769
Email: info@napusa.org
Website: http://www.napusa.org
The association is for programmers, developers, consultants, and other professionals and students in the computer industry. It provides information and resources for members, including articles, certification, events, and more.

Abraham, Nikhil. *Coding for Dummies*. Hoboken, NJ: John Wiley & Sons, 2016.

Abramovitz, Melissa. *Cybersecurity Analyst* (Cutting Edge Careers). San Diego, CA: ReferencePoint Press, 2017.

Bedell, J. M. *So, You Want to Be a Coder? The Ultimate Guide to a Career in Programming, Video Game Creation, Robotics, and More!* New York, NY: Aladdin, 2016.

Harmon, Daniel E. *Cyber Attacks, Counterattacks, and Espionage* (Cryptography: Code Making and Code Breaking). New York, NY: Rosen Publishing, 2017.

Kamberg, Mary-Lane. *Cybersecurity: Protecting Your Identity and Data* (Digital and Information Literacy). New York, NY: Rosen Publishing, 2018.

Kassnoff, David. *What Degree Do I Need to Pursue a Career in Information Technology & Information Systems?* New York, NY: Rosen Publishing, 2014.

Lowe, Doug. *Java All-in-One for Dummies*. Hoboken, NJ: John Wiley & Sons, 2014.

Matthes, Eric. *Python Crash Course: A Hands-On, Project-Based Introduction to Programming*. San Francisco, CA: No Starch Press, 2015.

Niver, Heather. *Careers for Tech Girls in Computer Science*. New York, NY: Rosen Publishing, 2014.

Payment, Simone. *Getting to Know Python! Code Power: A Teen Programmer's Guide*. New York, NY: Rosen Publishing, 2014.

Porterfield, Jason. *White and Black Hat Hackers* (Cryptography: Code Making and Code Breaking). New York, NY: Rosen Publishing, 2017.

Accenture.com. "2017 Cost of Cyber Crime." https://www.accenture.com.

Balut, Dawid. "How to Become a Security Expert with Zero Experience." *Forbes*, May 2, 2018. https://www.forbes.com.

Bureau of Labor Statistics. "Information Security Analyst." *Occupational Outlook Handbook*. https://www.bls.gov.

CareerCast. "Best Jobs of 2016: Information Security Analyst." https://www.careercast.com.

CyberDegrees.org. "Become a Cryptographer or Cryptanalyst." https://www.cyberdegrees.org/jobs/cryptographer.

Fandos, Nicholas. "NSA Summer Camp: More Hacking than Hiking." *New York Times*, July 17, 2015. https://www.nytimes.com/2015/07/18/us/nsa-summer-camp-hacking-cyber-defense.html.

Francis, Ryan. "Computer Forensics Follows the Bread Crumbs Left by Perpetrators." CSO Online, May 8, 2017. https://www.csoonline.com/article/3192348/security/computer-forensics-follows-the-bread-crumbs-left-by-perpetrators.html.

Gupta, Upasana. "The Cryptology Profession: Its Evolution, Growth, Skill Set and Career Prospects." Bank Info Security, May 28, 2009. http://www.bankinfosecurity.com/cryptology-profession-its-evolution-growth-skill-set-career-prospects-a-1500.

Haag, Michael. "Security Architect Lessons: What I Learned Managing and Assessing Cyber Risk at a Fortune 200." Red Canary, April 25, 2018. http://

www.redcanary.com/blog/security-architect-lessons
-learned-managing-assessing.

IEEE Cyber Security. "Christof Paar on Why
Cryptography Is Key for Automotive Cybersecurity."
June 28, 2017. https://cybersecurity.ieee
.org/blog/2017/06/28/christof-paar-on-why
-cryptography-is-key-for-automotive-cybersecurity.

Kauflin, Jeff. "The Fast-Growing Job with a Huge Skills
Gap: Cyber Security." *Forbes*, March 16, 2017.
https://www.forbes.com.

Keirsten Brager.tech. "#WeCyberToo: Tiffany L. Smith,
Security Analyst, Fortune 100 Company." https://
keirstenbrager.tech/tiffanysmith.

Korolov, Maria. "What It Takes to Become an
Application Security Engineer." CSO Online, April 5,
2017. https://www.csoonline.com.

Magee, Tamlin. "What Is Penetration Testing? Meet
the Security Pros Breaking Into Your Business for
Cash." *Computerworld UK*, March 9, 2017. https://
www.computerworlduk.com/security
/what-is-penetration-testing-3637534.

Owens, Jeremy. "The Equifax Data Breach in One
Chart." MarketWatch, September 10, 2018. http://
www.marketwatch.com/story
/the-equifax-data-breach-in-one-chart-2018-09-07.

Risen, Tom. "Lawmakers Demand Cybersecurity
Reform After Sony Hack." *U.S. News & World Report*,
December 19, 2014. https://www.usnews.com
/news/articles/2014/12/19/lawmakers-demand
-cybersecurity-reform-after-sony-hack.

Roberts, Jeff John, and Adam Lashinsky, "Hacked: How
Business Is Fighting Back Against the Explosion

in Cybercrime." *Fortune*, June 22, 2017. http://
fortune.com/2017/06/22/cybersecurity-business
-fights-back.

Robinson, Rick. "38 Million Reasons to Use
Cryptography for Business." Security Intelligence,
November 11, 2013. https://securityintelligence
.com/reasons-encryption-cryptography-for-business.

Roufa, Timothy. "What It's like to Work as a Digital
Forensic Examiner." Balance Careers, May 1, 2018.
https://www.thebalancecareers.com/what-it-s-like
-to-work-as-a-digital-forensic-examiner-974889.

Stupple, Laura. "A Day in the Life of a Cyber Security
Engineer." Learning People.https://blog
.learningpeople.co.uk/a-day-in-the-life-of-a-cyber
-security-engineer.

Tabriz, Parisa. "So, You Want to Work in Security?"
freeCodeCamp, July 28, 2016. https://medium
.freecodecamp.org.

*U.S. News & World Report*. "Information Security
Analyst." https://money.usnews.com/careers
/best-jobs/information-security-analyst/reviews.

Welles, Tim. "Reflections of an Intern: My
Cybersecurity Career Path." Sword & Shield, August
22, 2017. https://www.swordshield
.com/2017/08/cybersecurity-career-path.

Williams, Jeff. "Building a Strong Foundation for
a Career in Cybersecurity Penetration Testing."
*Forbes*, April 12, 2018. https://www.forbes.com
/sites/forbestechcouncil.

# INDEX

# ABOUT THE AUTHOR

Carla Mooney is a graduate of the University of Pennsylvania. Before becoming an author, she spent several years working in finance as an accountant. Today, she writes for young people and is the author of many books for young adults and children. Mooney enjoys learning about new technologies and the impact they will have on different industries and the average digital user.

# PHOTO CREDITS

Cover Erik Isakson/Tetra Images/Getty Images; back cover, pp. 4–5 (background) nadla/E+/Getty Images; p. 5 (inset) CasarsaGuru/E+/Getty Images; pp. 8, 17, 26, 35, 44, 53, 60 (background) Pasko Maksim/Shutterstock.com, (circuit pattern) Titima Ongkantong/Shutterstock.com; p. 9 sitthiphong/Shutterstock.com; p. 11 Erik Isakson/Blend Images/Getty Images; p. 14 Yurich/Shutterstock.com; pp. 18, 21, 29 © AP Images; p. 24 Monkey Business Images/Shutterstock.com; p. 27 tuthelens/Shutterstock.com; pp. 31, 54 Gorodenkoff/Shutterstock.com; p. 36 Oleksiy Mark/Shutterstock.com; p. 39 PR Image Factory/Shutterstock.com; p. 41 Photofusion/UIG/Getty Images; pp. 45, 50 Bloomberg/Getty Images; p. 47 South_agency/E+/Getty Images; p. 56 nd3000/Shutterstock.com; p. 58 REDPIXEL.PL/Shutterstock.com; p. 61 antb/Shutterstock.com; p. 62 Ujjwal Swami/Shutterstock.com; p. 67 Rawpixel.com/Shutterstock.com; additional background textures and graphics Verticalarray/Shutterstock.com (p. 1), Toria/Shutterstock.com (p. 3).

Design: Michael Moy; Layout: Nicole Russo-Duca; Photo Researcher: Karen Huang